101

Ways to Save the
Planet

Deborah Underwood

Raintree

www.raintreepublishers.co.uk
Visit our website to find out
more information about
Raintree books.

To order:
☎ Phone 0845 6044371
🖹 Fax +44 (0) 1865 312263
📧 Email myorders@raintreepublishers.co.uk

Customers from outside the UK please telephone +44 1865 312262

Raintree is an imprint of Capstone Global Library
Limited, a company incorporated in England and Wales
having its registered office at 7 Pilgrim Street, London,
EC4V 6LB – Registered company number: 6695582

Edited by Andrew Farrow and Vaarunika Dharmapala
Designed by Richard Parker
Picture research by Ruth Blair
Originated by Capstone Global Library Ltd
Printed and bound in China by South China Printing
  Company Ltd

ISBN 978 1 406 21750 6 (hardback)
15 14 13 12 11
10 9 8 7 6 5 4 3 2 1

ISBN 978 1 406 21778 0 (paperback)
16 15 14 13 12
10 9 8 7 6 5 4 3 2 1

British Library Cataloguing in Publication Data
Underwood, Deborah.
101 ways to save the planet.
333.7'2-dc22
A full catalogue record for this book is available
from the British Library.

Acknowledgments
We would like to thank the following for permission
to reproduce photographs: Alamy pp 37 (Andrew
Rubtsov), 46 (Bruce Coleman Inc.); Corbis pp 7
(Tim Klein/Aurora Photos), 12 (Bloomimage), 15
(Artiga Photo), 16 (Toby Melville/Reuters), 17 (Image
Source), 22 (Construction Photography), 29 (Randy
Faris), 41 (Ted Dayton Photography/Beateworks), 42
(Mika), 44 (Steven Kazlowski/Science Faction), 48 (Tim
Pannell), 51 (Oliver Rossi); Getty Images p 32 (George
Pimentel/WireImage); iStockphoto pp 4 (Aldo Murillo),
21 (Vikram Raghuvanshi Photography), 24 (Joe
Potato Photo), 34 (seraficus), 35 (Tomasz Pietryszek),
39 (Amber Antozak), 49 (Sian Cox); Shutterstock
pp 7 (Petr Mašek), 9 (Jacob Kearns), **11 top** (Leonid
Shcheglov), **11 bottom** (Christina Richards), 13
(LianeM), 19 (Mihai Simonia), 20 (Antonio V. Oquias),
25 (IA98), 27 (Adrian Britton), 30 (Arvind Balaraman),
31 (oliveromg), 33 (mikeledray), 36 (auremar), 45
(Matsonashvili Mikhail).

Cover photograph of a teenage girl hugging a
tree, reproduced with permission of Getty Images
(Thinkstock).

Every effort has been made to contact copyright holders
of material reproduced in this book. Any omissions will
be rectified in subsequent printings if notice is given to
the publisher.

Contents

In order to protect the privacy of individuals featured in case studies, some names have been changed.

Words appearing in the text in bold, **like this**, are explained in the Glossary.

Introduction

We live on a pretty wonderful planet. Earth has adorable pandas, tropical islands, stunning mountains, and land to grow the food we need. Unfortunately, though, Earth also has some big problems. Even more unfortunately, these problems are the fault of our very own species.

We humans have done some amazing things in the last few centuries. We've cured diseases, built computers, and harnessed the power of electricity. But in the process, we've made a bit of a mess of our planet.

People affect the planet in many ways, both good and bad.

listen up!

Is it getting hot in here? Unfortunately the answer is "yes". Earth's average surface temperature has increased by about 0.74°C (1.33°F) in the last 100 years. That's a big deal. Higher temperatures mean melting ice caps, weird weather, and rising sea levels, amongst other things. Scientists believe temperatures are rising because of things we humans are doing, such as burning **fossil fuels**.

What's that?
Fossil fuels are materials such as oil, coal, and natural gas. They formed within Earth from the remains of plants and animals that lived millions of years ago.

Pollution problems

Humans burn fuels and use chemicals that cause air pollution – poisonous stuff that gets into the air and harms people and other animals. Chemicals in the air also cause **acid rain**, which can harm soil, crops, and forests. It can even eat away at buildings.

Quiz

What does it mean when you're green?

a) you're very envious

b) you're very inexperienced at something

c) you're trying to help the **environment**.

Find out the truth!

Actually, all these answers could be right. But we think the most important one is **c**. *Green* can also be used to describe environmentally friendly products, services, or businesses.

Q What does *eco* mean?

A *Eco* is a prefix that means "environmental". For example, *eco-friendly* means "environmentally friendly".

Population growth

In 1804 the world's population was about one billion people. Now it's over six billion! That means there are six times as many people living on our planet as there were just a couple of hundred years ago.

It's the same as if there were four people living in your house and then there were twenty-four. Do you think that might cause problems? (Can you imagine the queue for the bathroom?!)

The world has a limited amount of some **resources** such as oil, water, and food. The more people on Earth, the more pressure we put on these resources, and the greater the danger of running short.

Q What's the big deal about water? You turn on the tap and it comes out, doesn't it?

A Not necessarily. There are about one billion people around the world who don't have access to clean drinking water. Even those of us who are lucky enough to have it need to be careful how much of it we use. There's only a certain amount of water in the world. We need to keep it clean and use it wisely.

Oops! The more people there are on the planet, the more rubbish we make. Some of that rubbish is plastic that will hang around for hundreds of years. A plastic planet is not exactly the best gift to give our great-great-great-great-grandchildren, is it...?

As people spread out on the planet, there are fewer resources available for our fellow Earthlings. When we cut down trees to make furniture or to free up land to grow food, we destroy other animals' **habitats**. When we pollute the oceans, the animals that live there suffer. The choices we make affect animals all over the world, from the Amazon to the Arctic. Many animal species are in danger of dying out forever because of human activities.

What's that?

A **habitat** is the place where an organism, such as an animal, lives.

So what can I do?

You can do a lot! What you do, what you eat, and what you buy can have a huge impact on the planet. You – yes, YOU! – can make the world a better place. Many environmentally friendly things you can do can make you healthier and happier, too. You may not be able to do all these things now, but if you do even some of them, you'll really be helping the planet. So roll up your sleeves and get ready to make a difference!

One person can make a big difference in the fight to save the planet.

Eating green

Our food choices affect lots of things: for example, the amounts of water and fuel we use up, the amount of rubbish we throw away, the amount of **pesticides** we put into the soil, not to mention how healthy we are. The good news is that making Earth-friendly food choices is an easy (and tasty) way to help the planet several times a day!

What's that?
A **pesticide** is a substance used to kill insects that may eat crops.

01 Eat **organic** food when you can. Non-organic food growers may use chemicals that harm the environment.

02 Plant a fruit and vegetable garden. Instead of driving to the supermarket and buying food that's been driven, flown, or shipped to your town, you can just go outside and pick your own.

03 When you buy packaged food, read the label. If a food is full of chemicals you can't pronounce, you might want to think twice about eating it. It may be unhealthy and it certainly won't be organic. Labels will also tell you if the food is organic or not.

04 Better still, avoid packaged food whenever you can.

05 Eat wholefoods (see quiz on page 9). They use up less energy to produce and are usually better for you.

06 Buy locally grown food. It takes much less fuel to transport local foods to your farmers' markets or local shop than to import food from other countries.

07 Eat fruit and vegetables in season. If you live in a big town or city and can buy strawberries during the dead of winter, you can bet that the strawberries were grown a long way away. (Strawberries don't grow well in freezing weather!)

Look for fruit and vegetables that are organic or locally grown. Or, better yet, both!

Quiz

What is a wholefood?

a) food with a hole in it, like a doughnut

b) food that you can't cut in half

c) food that is either unprocessed or has been processed very little.

Find out the truth!

The answer is **c**. Brown rice is a wholefood, because very little is done to it before it ends up on your supermarket shelf. An apple is a wholefood, too, along with all whole fruits and veggies.

But white rice is a processed food because the outer part of the rice has been polished away. Tomato ketchup is processed, because the tomatoes have been cooked, made into sauce, and packaged. Processing food uses energy, so eating wholefoods can save energy.

Factory farming

Today a lot of the meat we buy comes from factory farms. These are places that rear huge numbers of animals in a relatively small space. Having so many animals in one place puts stress on the land. For one thing, big herds or flocks of animals make a lot of waste. Getting rid of the waste from hundreds of thousands of animals can be a big problem.

Cramming all these animals together also allows diseases to spread quickly from one animal to another. Furthermore, animals in factory farms have horrible lives. For example, chickens are often crammed together in small cages. Imagine how you would feel being trapped in a crowded lift forever.

Quiz

What is a food chain?

a) a necklace made of Brussels sprouts

b) a way of showing how nutrients pass from one living thing to another

c) something you use to lock your lunchbox to your desk so no one will steal it.

Find out the truth!

The answer is b. It's good to eat low on the food chain, that is, to eat plants instead of animals. If you eat a burger made from a cow, you're not just eating the meat. In a way, you're also eating all the plants that the cow ever ate. You're also using up all the water that the cow drank, and all the water that it took to grow the plants the cow ate. If you only eat plants, you use up less resources.

These turkeys are crowded together in a factory farm. They barely have room to move.

Where does your food come from?

There are still some smaller farms that rear animals. These farms are not as hard on the planet as factory farms, and the animals raised on these farms may be treated more humanely. If you want to eat animal products, look for meat, cheese, milk, and eggs from these farms.

Oops! According to a United Nations report, rearing livestock is responsible for 18 per cent of greenhouse gases (the gases that are causing climate change) in the atmosphere. That's more than cars, buses, and other forms of transport.

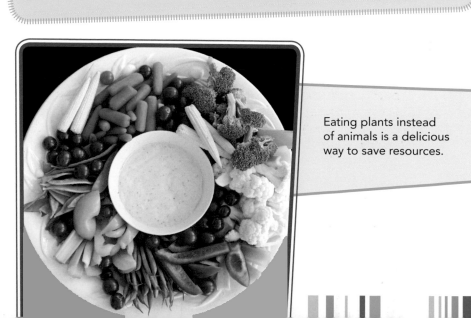

Eating plants instead of animals is a delicious way to save resources.

Green eating on the go

You probably eat many of your meals away from home, either at school or in restaurants or cafés. Every meal out is an opportunity to create less litter! Here are some tips:

08 Take your own mug with you when you buy coffee or tea on the run.

09 Use reusable containers for lunch. Put them in your rucksack after you've eaten so you remember to take them home and wash them.

10 Bringing food from home almost always creates less litter than buying food because of all the packaging shops use. It saves you money, too.

11 Are you going to that restaurant that serves mammoth portions? Take your own container along, so you can bring the leftovers home with you.

Reuseable containers help make lunchtime Earth-friendly.

Break it down! Composting basics

Instead of tossing fruit and vegetable scraps into the rubbish bin, **compost** them! Materials such as garden waste and food scraps break down over time. Gradually they turn into a rich, dark substance called **humus**, which is part of soil. When the humus is added to a garden, it makes the soil healthier.

Composting idea 1
A compost pile: this is the
simplest way of composting. You
just put garden waste in a pile in
your garden. If you turn the
compost to mix up the pile, you
can add food scraps, too. If you
don't turn the compost, the food
may attract pests.

Composting idea 2
A compost bin: you use a container to
hold the compost. The container can be
simply some fencing or mesh formed
into a circle or square. Or you can buy a
compost bin at a garden centre. Some
bins rotate, allowing you to turn the
compost without using a garden fork.

Composting idea 3
A wormery: worms are amazing composters! You put red
worms in a special container, along with bedding material,
such as shredded newspaper, along with your food scraps.
Before long, the worms make a rich compost that's great for
gardens. You can order red worms online, or if you live in the
country you may be able to get them from a local farmer.

More ways to eat green when you're out

12 Unless you're planning to pour your drink over your head, you probably don't need 20 serviettes. Only take what you need.

13 Pack reusable eating utensils with your school lunch so you don't have to use throw-away plastic ones.

14 If you take snacks to school in a plastic bag, take the bag home and reuse it.

15 Do you really need that plastic lid on your coke, tea, or coffee? If you're planning a roller coaster ride while you're drinking it, by all means get one. But if you're just going to sit in a café, you probably don't need it (unless you're expecting an earthquake).

16 Better yet, if you're staying in the restaurant or café, ask for a real cup rather than a plastic or paper one.

17 Use cloth napkins. Tuck one into your rucksack or keep it in your locker. Remember to take it home to wash it once in a while!

18 Unless you are in a country where the water is unsafe to drink, try not to buy bottled water. It creates more waste. Tap water will quench your thirst just as effectively.

Bottled water: think before you drink

People buy bottled water for lots of reasons. They may think it's healthier or more convenient, or perhaps they think it looks cool to be seen carrying a famous brand of bottled water.

Bottled water can cost thousands of times more than tap water. So, surely the water inside must be better for you than water straight from the tap? Wrong! In fact, in some places the rules about what can go into bottled water are weaker than the rules for tap water.

Bottled water is creating a huge plastic waste problem. Worldwide, over 2.5 million tonnes (2.7 million tons) of plastic are used each year to bottle water. Most water bottles never get recycled. Even if they do, plastic recycling isn't as efficient as glass or metal recycling.

There's a simple solution: buy a stainless steel water bottle and fill it from the tap. The bottles come in lots of sizes and colours, so you can pick one that suits your personality. The important thing is that you're keeping lots of plastic bottles out of **landfill** sites.

When you work out, help the planet get healthy, too. Use a stainless steel water bottle.

Green glamour

You now know that what you eat and what you drink can help the planet. So can what you wear.

Most clothes you buy are:

- manufactured (which uses energy and creates waste)
- shipped to shops and warehouses (which uses energy and creates pollution and waste)
- sold in shops (which uses energy and creates pollution if you use a car or bus to get there); OR
- ordered online and shipped to your home (which uses energy and creates pollution and waste).

Notice a pattern here? Next time you're desperate to buy your seventh purple-striped jumper, think about the energy involved in making the clothes and getting them to you.

What's more, manufacturing clothes can be pretty tough on the planet. Polyester fabric is made from fossil fuels. Cotton is a natural fibre, but some cotton growers use lots of chemicals on their crops. Petroleum, a fossil fuel, is used to make many fabric dyes.

Fortunately there are ways to dress that have less impact on the planet, but look just as good.

Laura Bailey is a model who supports eco-fashion, that is, clothes that are produced in a way that has as little impact on Earth as possible.

Don't toss out the clothes you're tired of. How about swapping them with your friends instead?

19 Sick of your clothes? Don't throw them out! Have a clothes-exchange party with your friends instead. Donate any leftovers to charity shops.

20 Instead of buying new clothes, search the racks in charity shops for cool retro fashions and quirky accessories. It's like a treasure hunt – you never know when you'll uncover an amazing vintage find.

21 Learn to knit. (Yes, boys can knit, too!) Unravel those old jumpers full of holes, and knit the wool into funky hats and loony, long scarves for yourself and your friends.

22 Teach yourself to sew and be your own fashion designer! If you have access to a sewing machine, you can chop, hack, and stitch your boring old clothes and transform them into something original and special. There are lots of books and magazines out there to help you with ideas.

23 Look around market stalls or fairs for unique and affordable clothes and accessories that have been made by local designers or craftspeople. Keep an eye open for fabulous, eco-friendly fabrics, such as organic cotton and hemp.

Fabulous fabric 1: bamboo

If you think bamboo is only food for pandas, think again! Bamboo can be turned into chopping boards, kitchen worktops, and clothes. Fabric made from bamboo is light and strong. Best of all, bamboo grows quickly and can be grown without pesticides. So buying and wearing bamboo clothes is a brilliant environmental move.

Fabulous fabric 2: spun plastic

Hmm … what to wear today … how about an old plastic bottle? Yes, old bottles made from PET (a type of plastic) can be turned into fibre strands, then woven into fabric. The fabric can be made into cosy fleece garments, blankets, and even carpets.

Oops!

Cotton is another fabulous fabric. After all, where would we be without our jeans? But by some estimates, more than 10 per cent of the world's pesticides and 25 per cent of its **insecticides** are dumped on – you guessed it – cotton crops. These pesticides can harm our soil and water, not to mention the people who work in or live near cotton fields.

However, you don't have to give up on this wonderful fabric. Many farmers are now growing organic cotton, which is much easier on the planet. So when you're shopping for clothes, look for organic cotton.

What's that?

An **insecticide** is a substance used to kill insects.

24 Reduce clothes washing. Okay, if you've just played a muddy game of football, your clothes are probably genuinely dirty. But what about that shirt you wore for only 45 minutes today? Don't toss it in the laundry basket. Put it back in the cupboard.

25 Only use the washing machine when you have a full load of clothes. Always try to wash clothes on a low temperature setting, for example 30°C (86°F). This saves the energy that would have been used to heat the water.

26 Some kinds of dry cleaning can be bad for the air and for your health. Many dry cleaners use a chemical called perchloroethylene that pollutes the air. One test showed that wearing dry-cleaned clothes just once a week can be a health risk. Luckily, some cleaners are now using **carbon dioxide** to clean clothes instead. Look for one of these eco-friendly cleaners if you have clothes that need to be dry-cleaned.

listen up!

You might use make-up. You definitely use soap (we hope). Keep an eye open for toiletries and cosmetics with little or no packaging. See if you can find bars of soap or shampoo that are sold without wrappers. Some toiletry and cosmetic companies run a refill scheme for their liquid products, such as shampoo and lotions. Use it! Also, look for products in recyclable metal tins, not plastic tubes.

Tackle that rubbish

You toss an old envelope into the rubbish bin, or throw a plastic bag away. You never see it again. So what's the problem?

The problem is that our rubbish doesn't magically disappear. It goes somewhere, even if we can't see it any more. The more of us there are on the planet, the more rubbish we produce. Our litter affects the lives of humans and other animals – and not in good ways.

Millions of tonnes of waste are added to landfill sites around the world every year.

Recycling is a good start to helping the planet. It turns old stuff into new stuff, and helps keep things out of landfill sites. But recycling isn't perfect. It uses energy. And some things can't be recycled easily, or at all.

That's where the three R's – *reduce, reuse, recycle* – come in. Recycling stuff is good. Reusing stuff is better. Reducing the amount of stuff you buy in the first place is best of all.

27 Be a dustbin detective. Take a look in the rubbish bins in your house. How much stuff in there could be composted or recycled? Look at what you're throwing away and work out the best ways to reduce the rubbish in your bins in the future.

28 When you go shopping with your family, take your own bags. It doesn't matter if they're reused plastic carrier bags or cloth bags. The point is to avoid getting a new bag. If you buy something you can carry easily, say "no" to a bag if the checkout assistant offers you one.

29 Do unwanted catalogues cascade through your letterbox? If there is a free phone number on the catalogue, call the company and ask them to remove your address from their mailing list. (Check with your parents first to make sure it's okay.)

Make your shopping trip Earth-friendly by taking along your own reuseable bag.

Eco-activity: trash test

Just for one day, make a list of everything you throw out or recycle. At the end of the day, look at your list. Are you surprised? After you've read this book, do the exercise again. Have you made changes that mean you're binning less stuff? Why not challenge a friend to a "trash-test": make lists on the same day and see who generates the least rubbish and recycling. The loser can take the winner out for an eco-friendly treat!

Oops!

"Downcycling" sounds like cycling down a hill. But it's what some people call plastic recycling. The glass bottles you recycle can be melted down and made into more bottles. A recycled aluminium can may become another aluminium can. This can happen over and over again.

But most of the time when plastic is recycled it loses quality. It can be recycled a limited number of times. What's more, most plastic is made from **non-renewable** fuels such as natural gas or oil.

Recycle plastic bottles if you can. Better yet, don't buy them in the first place.

Q Why should you recycle?

A Recycling some things saves a lot of energy. By some estimates, making a drinks can from recycled aluminium saves 95 per cent of the energy that it would take to make the can from aluminium ore. Even though recycling plastic isn't the most efficient process in the world, it still keeps plastic out of our landfill sites, which are filling up fast.

Q Doesn't my rubbish break down in the landfill site?

 A Maybe, maybe not. Some things, such as plastic bags, stick around for a long time, possibly hundreds of years. Also, even banana peels and paper need oxygen in order to **decompose**. In some landfill sites, things are packed tightly on top of each other, and some landfills are sealed. In either case, if oxygen can't reach the waste material the rubbish can't break down.

30 Recycle paper. This goes without saying. Put paper in the recycling bin, not the rubbish bin.

31 Instead of recycling paper with one blank side, reuse it. You may be able to print on the blank side. Or stack the papers blank-side-up and make notepads. Once both sides are used, then recycle it.

32 Don't drop litter. No one likes wading through rubbish while walking down the street.

33 Donate old toys and clothes to a good charity. You'll be helping other people and cutting down on waste.

34 Some waste is very **toxic**. The mercury in thermometers is poisonous and has a poisonous vapour. If you break a thermometer, don't try to clear it up yourself. Tell an adult immediately.

listen up!

You're in a public toilet. You've washed your hands and they're wet. Do you really need to dry them with a paper towel or an electric hand-dryer? Might we suggest you join the Dry-Your-Hands-On-Your-Jeans Club? All you need to do is – you guessed it – dry your hands on your jeans, or shake them dry. Think how much paper and energy would be saved if everyone did this! Granted, you won't want to do it when you're wearing your very best clothes or if you know your jeans are not that clean. But most of the time it works just fine. Give it a try!

35 Recycle your batteries. This is an important one. Batteries contain poisons that can leak into the soil. Take your used batteries to a place that can recycle them. Better still, buy rechargeable batteries.

36 Recycle your old mobile phone. Mobiles don't just take up space in landfills, they also contain toxic substances. Some places will pay cash for your old phone. Others take your phone and give it to someone who needs it.

37 Instead of buying a CD in a box, purchase MP3 files of the music you want. This will also save on potential plastic recycling. (Remember, you must pay for most music you download or you will find yourself on the wrong side of the law and may end up with a hefty fine.)

So you've recycled your paper. A company has turned that paper into a recycled-paper product, such as a pad of writing paper or a pack of Christmas cards. What's next? Someone needs to buy the recycled-paper product! If companies can't sell recycled products, they'll lose interest in making them. So when you have a choice, try to buy recycled stuff.

listen up!

Green giving

38 Get creative when you're wrapping gifts. Instead of buying expensive gift wrap, try using old wallpaper samples, or even newspaper tied up with bright fabric strips. You could also use a pretty scarf or a napkin. You could even make a reusable gift bag from fabric.

If you use unusual materials to wrap presents, you can make them unique and special, as well as green.

Do you have an animal-mad friend?
You could adopt a pig from an animal
sanctuary in their name.

39 Give time, not stuff. Instead of giving a material present that will end up in a landfill site, give the gift of your time. Make a certificate saying you'll babysit, or help with some gardening.

40 Bake your own presents. Cakes, biscuits, and breads make lovely gifts for most people. And they won't end up in a landfill like that plastic gnome you nearly bought.

41 Give an experience. Is your friend dying to see a particular film or gig? Tickets would make a great present. Or offer to take your friend on an eco-friendly picnic.

42 Give a gorilla or a pig! "Adopt" an animal at an animal sanctuary. Your friend will get a photo of his or her animal, as well as the satisfaction of helping an animal survive.

43 Give a donation in your friend's name to another type of charity. Is your friend concerned about world hunger, or saving rainforests, or rescuing dogs and cats? There's a charity for nearly every concern. (See page 54 for some suggestions, and look online for others.)

Make your school Earth-friendly

You probably spend a lot of time at school. A lot of what you buy is probably for school, too - paper, pens, notebooks, and so on. So school is a terrific opportunity to take planet-friendly action.

Take a look around your school with your new, improved eco-eyes. Are the rubbish bins full of paper that could be recycled? Are the canteen bins full of wasted food? Do lights get left on in classrooms when no one's inside?

Do you have any suggestions about how your school can become more Earth-friendly? Great! The next step is to get your ideas to the people who can change things. Suggest to your teacher that growing a vegetable garden would be a great class project. If your school has a student council, why not run for it and share your ideas with others? Here are some tips to get you started:

44 Save some wood by buying recycled pencils. You can get pencils made from recycled newspapers, recycled jeans – even recycled money!

45 Buy refillable pens instead of disposable plastic pens.

46 Work with your teachers to organize a litter-free day, or a litter-free lunch day at school. Ask the school caretaker how many bags of litter your school makes on a normal day. Compare that with the litter-free day.

47 Ask your school canteen to go tray-less. One study has shown that washing canteen trays can use up to two litres (almost half a gallon) of water. Multiply that by the number of lunches on trays your school canteen serves each year and you can see how much water could be saved! One university in the United States saved 11,356 litres (2,498 gallons) of water each day by going tray-less.

48 Ask what happens to leftover food from the canteen. Is it thrown away? If it is, find out if there's a way the food could be donated to feed homeless people instead.

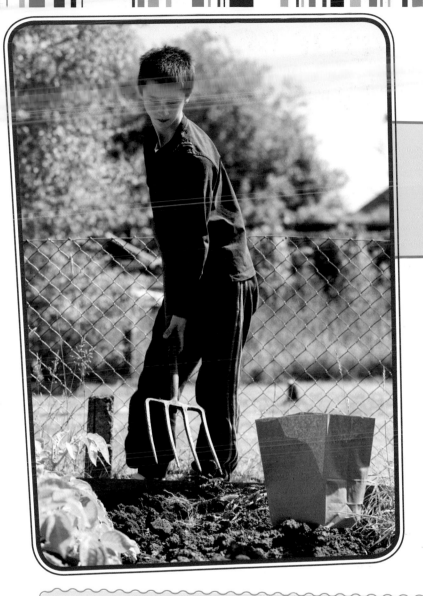

Planting a class vegetable garden is a fun project that everyone can get involved in.

Part of what makes school fun are activities such as sporting events and dances. If you're helping to organize an event, think about ways to make it easier on the planet.

Serve veggie hotdogs instead of factory-farmed meat. Ask people to bring their own plates, cups, and utensils. Put out bins for waste that can be recycled or composted, as well as rubbish bins. If there's an admissions charge, offer a discount for people who walk, cycle, or take public transport to the event.

Being green: a class act

49 Harness the brainpower of other kids in your school. Have a contest for the best eco-friendly school ideas. Each class can come up with something, or individuals can compete against each other. You'll end up with a lot of great ideas that your school can consider doing.

50 Once your school has come up with some brilliant environmental ideas, ask your head teacher if you can share them with another school in your area. Perhaps that school will have some ideas for your school to use, too!

51 You know how much paper flies around at school: handouts, tests, homework, notes to your parents, notes from your parents – you get the idea. Find out if your school uses recycled paper. If it doesn't, suggest that it does. Even if that doesn't work, you can still take charge of your own paper use by buying recycled paper and notebooks, and wasting as little paper as you can.

52 Make recycling bins for your classroom. Get creative! Can you make them from used cardboard, or from something else that would otherwise be recycled or thrown out? Once the bins are ready, make sure there's a company that collects your school's recycling. If there isn't, talk to your teacher. Perhaps arranging for collection of your school's recyclables would be another good class project!

listen up!

Environmental awareness is big business these days; so big that some companies stretch the truth about just how eco-friendly they really are. This is called "greenwashing".

For example, a company that makes dangerous pesticides might boast about how its bottles are made from recycled plastic. Well, the bottle bit is great, but it's not exactly an Earth-friendly product if it's still full of poisons that end up in the air or water!

Start a class discussion about greenwashing. Take a look at some products that claim to be green and discuss whether you think they really are or not.

It's important to recycle whenever you can. Recycling helps to save resources.

Super-green schools

Lots of school buildings are getting green makeovers! The Fulston Manor School in Kent has solar panels on its roof. The panels use energy from the Sun to make electricity for the school.

Be water-wise

Every living thing, from a potted plant to a person, needs water to survive. If you look at the picture of Earth below, there seems to be water almost everywhere. Oceans and seas cover over 70 per cent of Earth's surface. There's even more water in streams, rivers, lakes, and glaciers. So is water one resource we don't need to worry about conserving (saving)?

No! Although we live on a watery planet, nearly all of Earth's water (over 97 per cent) is salt water that we can't drink. Another two per cent is frozen in glaciers and polar ice caps. So less than one per cent of Earth's water is available for our use. We need to do two things: save water, and keep the water we have clean.

Earth's oceans are full of salt water, but drinkable water is a rare resource.

53 Turn off the taps while you're brushing your teeth instead of letting the water run. If you brush your teeth twice a day (and of course you DO, don't you?), this will save about 30 litres (6.5 gallons) of water a day.

54 Be a drip detective. Check your taps at home for leaks. Put a few drops of food colouring in your toilet cistern and don't flush the toilet for at least 15 minutes. If you see coloured water in the toilet bowl, you know there's a leak. If you notice a dripping tap when you're out and about, tell the management.

55 Have shorter showers. It's okay, you can still sing in the shower – just choose shorter songs!

56 Don't use the toilet to dispose of tissues. Drop tissues in the rubbish bin instead. There's no need to waste water every time you toss a tissue into the loo.

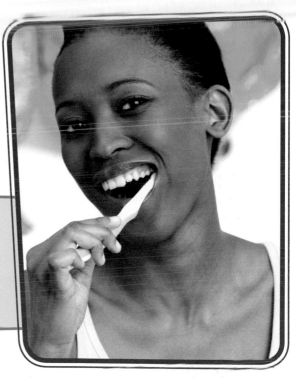

Don't let clean water flow down the drain. Turn off the tap while you brush.

Quiz

Test your water IQ

a) How much water does a full bath use?

b) How much water does a five-minute shower use?

c) How much water does the average person in the United Kingdom use daily?

Find out the truth!

a) 265 litres (70 gallons)
b) 38–95 litres (10–25 gallons)
c) 150 litres (40 gallons) per day

Go with the low-flow

Many homes and businesses have low-flow taps and showerheads. Less water comes out, but they work just as well. There are also toilets with two different flushes: the one for solid waste uses more water than the one for liquid waste. If your family is renovating a kitchen or bathroom, suggest that the adults consider low-flow fixtures.

57 Are you fond of cold, refreshing glasses of water? Keep a jug of water in the fridge instead of letting the tap run until it's cold.

58 Put the plug in the bathtub before you turn on the water for your bath.

59 Instead of using the hose to clean your patio, paths, or driveway, sweep them with a broom.

true story

Planet hero: Ryan Hreljac

When Ryan Hreljac was six years old, he learned that people in Africa were dying because they didn't have clean water. Ryan wanted to do something about it. He managed to raise some money and used it to build a well in Uganda. Ryan didn't stop there. Today the Ryan's Well Foundation is responsible for getting clean water to over half a million people. If a six-year-old can start something this big, think about what *you* can do!

60 Wash the family car or your bike with water in a bucket, instead of turning on a hose and letting it run. Better still, find a car wash that recycles the water it uses. Remember, any detergent you use to wash the car at home may end up in the sea.

61 Don't let water run while you wash the dishes. If you have two sinks, fill up one with washing water and one with rinsing water.

Oops!

The Great Pacific Garbage Patch is a huge mass of waste floating in the Pacific Ocean. It is made up of a lot of pieces of plastic – and when we say a lot of plastic, we mean *a lot*. One study found that the Garbage Patch averages over one third of a million pieces of plastic per square kilometre. It is thought by some to cover an area more than two and a half times the size of the United Kingdom.

Our plastic waste is causing big problems for the ocean and the animals that live in it. Animals can die when they eat the plastic, or when they get tangled up in it. One study estimated that over 40,000 northern fur seals in the Bering Sea die every year when they get tangled in plastic. And that's just one species, and one location.

Fishy issues

People used to think that they could catch as many fish as they wanted because the sea would always have enough. Now we know that isn't true. **Overfishing** has become a big problem.

Why? Well, these days fishing is no longer done by small groups of people with modest-sized nets or fishing rods. Now huge boats can catch tonnes of fish with a single scoop of their enormous nets.

When fish are scooped up, other animals get trapped in the big nets as well. These animals, called by-catch, die, too. Dolphins, sea turtles, and seals are all animals that get killed as by-catch.

Fish farming

People have begun rearing fish on fish farms. Oyster and mussel farms don't do much damage to the environment, but some fish, such as salmon, are reared in pens in or near the sea. If fish are crowded together, disease can easily spread amongst them. Also, lots of fish means lots of fish waste, so the farms can pollute the seawater.

What's that?

Overfishing means taking too many fish from one area.

Some farmed fish are raised in tanks, but others live in large cages by the sea.

More ways to keep water clean

62 If you notice that the family car is leaking oil, tell an adult. Oil on the ground gets washed down drains, and then into lakes, rivers, and the sea. Just a few litres of engine oil can pollute millions of litres of water.

63 Use safer cleaning products. You can scrub a sink with bicarbonate of soda or polish furniture with beeswax. A mix of vinegar and water in a spray bottle makes a great glass-cleaner.

64 Reduce pesticide use in the garden. You can make sprays that kill certain pests by mixing water with garlic or salt (look online for recipes). Ladybirds like to eat pests called aphids. What would you rather have floating around in your garden: lovely ladybirds or toxic chemicals?

65 Clean up after pets. Pet waste will pollute water if rainwater carries it into streams and lakes.

Ladybirds will eat up garden pests.

Spare the air

Take a deep breath, then let it out slowly. Ahhh ... Doesn't that feel good? We wouldn't survive long without fresh air. It gives our bodies the oxygen we need in order to function.

But there's a lot of stuff around that can pollute our air. Air pollution comes from all sorts of places: factories, cars and buses, power plants, cigarettes, and even certain kinds of paints and glues. In some countries, air quality has improved in the last 20 years. This is partly because of tougher laws against pollution. But in other places, the air is getting worse.

We need to protect Earth's air supply. Polluted air is not good for any of the animals on Earth, including humans. Air pollution is even changing the world's climate. So let's start the clean-up!

Oops!

Acid rain is what you get when pollutants make water in the air more acidic than usual. When the acid rain falls to Earth, it can harm plants and animals. It can even eat away at statues and buildings. Car exhaust fumes and burning fossil fuels contribute to acid rain.

Cycling is a form of transport and exercise all rolled into one!

66 Don't smoke. Smoking puts pollution into the air, not to mention into your body. Who needs that?

67 Try to use public transport instead of using a car.

68 Encourage your family to start up a carpool with friends. It saves fuel, and makes the journey more fun!

69 Cycle or walk to school. If it's too far, ask whoever drives you to drop you off about one kilometre and a half away from school (if it's safe). You'll get some great exercise and save a little petrol.

This velomobile will keep your homework dry in the rain. Your head sticks out but the rest of your body is inside!

listen up!

Sometimes there's an all-too-familiar problem with riding your bike. It's called rain! Arriving at school in a soggy, dripping mess doesn't exactly get your day off to a great start. That's where the velomobile comes in. A velomobile is an environmentally friendly pedal-powered car that's enclosed (so no problem with raindrops making your sandwiches soggy). There are not many on the road at the moment, but who knows? As people look for ways to stop climate change, pedal cars may become the next big thing.

Changing climate

Why is Earth heating up? It's partly because of something called the enhanced greenhouse effect. Greenhouses are great places to grow plants. They trap heat from the Sun, so the temperature inside the greenhouse is warmer than the temperature outside.

Certain gases, such as carbon dioxide, surround Earth and trap the Sun's heat like the glass walls of a greenhouse. Without this greenhouse effect, Earth would be so cold that we couldn't survive. When we burn fossil fuels, however, more greenhouse gases are released into the air. These extra gases are making Earth's temperature rise.

What's that?
Deforestation means the cutting down of trees.

Deforestation adds to the problem. Trees store carbon dioxide. Burning a tree releases carbon dioxide, a greenhouse gas, into the atmosphere. Plus the tree is no longer around to pull carbon dioxide from the air.

70 Plant a tree. Ask if you can plant one in your garden, or ask your teacher if your class can plant some trees in your neighbourhood as a class project.

71 Get a houseplant. Even a small plant can get rid of carbon dioxide and toxins. Spider plants, English ivy, and gerbera daisies are some good choices. If you have pets, make sure the plants you buy are not toxic to animals.

72 If you celebrate Christmas, get a living Christmas tree. After the holidays you can plant it outside. And you'll save a tree from being cut down.

Plants are not just nice to look at – they're natural air cleaners! They use carbon dioxide and light from the Sun to make food and oxygen. They can even filter toxic chemicals out of the air.

listen up!

73 If you buy a cut Christmas tree, see if you can recycle it. Some local councils will pick up old trees, or you can compost it with your garden waste.

74 Learn about the world's rainforests. These lush tropical forests found near Earth's equator make a lot of our oxygen, and use up a lot of carbon dioxide. They are also home to thousands of different kinds of animals. Do some rainforest research and find out about ways you can help protect these important forests.

Plants make oxygen, and they're nice to look at, too. Why not have a planting party with your friends?

true story

Planet hero: Wangari Maathai

Wangari Maathai is a Kenyan woman who started the Green Belt Movement, an organization that helps people and the environment. The Green Belt Movement has over 600 community networks in Kenya, and is responsible for the planting of over 30 million trees!

Conserving power

You walk into your kitchen, flick a switch, and the lights come on. You open the fridge and take out some juice. It's cold. You press a button and your computer comes on. Whether it's electrical power, natural gas power, or another type, we rely on power every day.

Have you ever thought about where your electricity comes from? Okay, we know about the socket in the wall! But before electrical power travels to your home or school, it needs to be produced.

Some electricity is made with the energy from flowing water. **Nuclear power** plants make some electricity. But most electricity in the United Kingdom is produced by factories that burn fossils fuels, such as coal. Earth has a limited supply of fossil fuels. They are non-renewable – eventually, we're going to run out of them.

So how can you help cut down on fossil fuel use? By conserving power! Fortunately, there are lots of easy ways to do that. Sometimes all you need to do is flick a switch!

Do fossil fuels really come from fossils?

Yes! Fossil fuels such as oil, natural gas, and coal formed from plants and animals that lived millions of years ago. When they died, their bodies broke down and were covered by sand, rock, and mud. Over time, they turned into fossil fuels. The plants and animals in most of our fossil fuels lived at least 300 million years ago. That's before dinosaurs roamed Earth.

Here's a bright idea: use compact fluorescent light bulbs!

75 Install compact fluorescent light bulbs (CFLs). They use much less power than standard, incandescent bulbs. An incandescent bulb uses four times as much power to produce the same amount of light as a CFL. CFLs last a lot longer, too.

76 Turn off the lights! If you're not hanging out in a room, flick the switch.

77 Keep your fridge and freezer full; that way, they use less energy. You can use this as an excuse to fill the freezer with ice cream, or you can just fill up plastic jugs with water and put them in the fridge.

78 Do you feel a *whoosh* of cool air when you open the fridge? For all the cold air that's whooshing out, there's an equal amount of warm air whooshing in. It needs to be cooled down, which takes energy. Decide what you want before opening the fridge door, and don't open it more than you need to.

Eco-exercise: have an unpowered hour!

When was the last time you and your family sat around together in the dark without the television on? Pick an hour when everyone's at home and agree not to use any power: no television, no computers, no lights, no switching on the electric kettle. You can light some candles, play a board game, maybe even (gasp!) talk to each other! You might like it so much that you choose to have an unpowered hour every week.

You don't need all the lights on to relax and have fun.

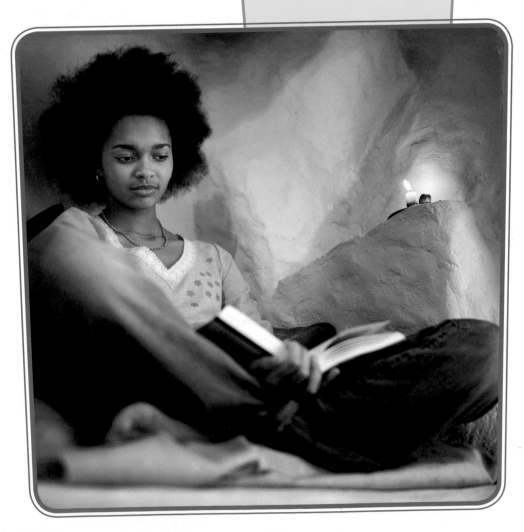

Renewable energy

It's likely that we will run out of fossil fuels one day. Luckily, there are also **renewable** energy sources. For instance, solar energy is renewable, because we're not going to run out of power from the Sun. Power made by water and wind is also renewable. So is power made from plants.

However, just because energy is renewable it doesn't necessarily mean it's good. Burning wood to heat your home uses a renewable resource, but it also pollutes the air. To keep Earth healthy, we are going to need energy sources that are both renewable *and* **sustainable**.

What's that?
Sustainable means something that doesn't harm Earth and won't run out, such as sunlight which can provide solar power.

79 Items such as computers pull a little bit of energy from the socket even when they're turned off. If you're going on holiday, unplug your computer, television, and other electrical appliances.

80 Get a solar-powered calculator.

81 Put a lid on it! If you're boiling a pan of water, cover it with a lid to prevent heat escaping and make it heat up faster.

82 Shut down your computer at night.

83 Microwave ovens can use less than half the energy of standard ovens, so microwaving a meal can be energy-smart.

84 Suggest to your family that you keep your home a little cooler in the winter by setting the central heating at a lower temperature. Put on a fleece or jumper and warm socks if you're cold. Just a few degrees can make a big difference in the amount of energy you save.

Fossil fuel in ... a box of crayons?

What do car and bike tyres, crayons, and plastic have in common? Believe it or not, they're all made from petroleum, a fossil fuel. Fossil fuels lurk in lots of everyday products. By using less stuff, you can help conserve fossil fuels.

Give animals a helping hand

Sometimes we humans behave as if we're the only animals on Earth. But the fact is we share our planet with millions of other species. When we pollute the water or the air, or destroy habitats, it affects the other animals, too.

One big problem for animals is habitat destruction. For example, lemurs are super-cool creatures that live only on the islands of Madagascar and Comoro, near Africa. Unfortunately, their forest homes are being cut down for **logging** and development. Many species of lemurs are already classified as **endangered species**.

Since we humans are responsible for these changes, we should give our fellow animals a helping hand when we can. Even small things you do can make life easier for our furry, feathered, and scaly animal friends.

listen up!

Climate change is affecting all the animals on Earth, even polar bears who live way up in the Arctic. Because the planet is warming, the ice on which the bears live is melting away. As the ice melts, the bears can get stranded on floating blocks of ice, unable to reach safety.

85 Don't flush cat poo down the toilet. It can carry organisms that make sea otters and other marine creatures ill. If you flush it away, the organisms can end up in the sea.

86 Snip the rings on plastic six-pack holders before you throw them away. Fish and birds can get caught in the rings and choke.

87 That lovely balloon drifting across the sky is going to end up somewhere, perhaps in the sea. Animals such as sea turtles can mistake balloons for jellyfish, eat them, and then die. So save animals by hanging on to your balloons.

88 Keep an eye open for plastic bags on the street and pick them up. Like balloons, plastic bags can kill animals that mistake them for food and eat them.

89 If your family wants a pet, adopt an animal from a local shelter. There are always plenty of great pets that need homes. Millions of animals are killed each year because there aren't enough homes for them. By saving a pet from a shelter, you're helping to stop this problem. Once you get your pet, be sure to have it spayed or neutered.

90 Cats roaming around outside are a nightmare for wild birds. If you have a cat, consider keeping it inside. This will keep your pet safe from other animals and cars, too. If you want your cat to roam free, a bell on the collar will give birds some warning so they can get away.

91 If you see someone mistreating an animal, tell an adult immediately.

92 The more people on the planet, the fewer the wild places left for animals to live. Raise money to donate to a group that protects animal habitats. Keep a corner of your garden wild to provide homes for butterflies and insects.

93 Get wise about animals, even ones that seem creepy or scary. Bats may look frightening (especially if you've seen too many vampire films), but one bat can eat 3,000 mosquitoes in one night! Predators such as sharks help to keep the oceans healthy. The more you know about how cool animals are, the more you'll want to protect them.

94 If you see an injured wild animal, call the RSPCA or your local wildlife rescue organization. They can tell you what to do to help it.

95 Never release a domestic animal into the wild. It may not be able to take care of itself, and it may cause problems for the animals that actually belong there.

Planet hero: Jane Goodall

When Jane Goodall was 23 years old, she travelled from the United Kingdom to Tanzania to study wild chimpanzees. Her work with chimpanzees made her famous, and also helped her understand that human activities such as logging are putting animals in danger. In 1991 Jane Goodall and 16 young people founded the Roots & Shoots programme. This scheme encourages kids to do things to help people, animals, and the environment. Today there are tens of thousands of Roots & Shoots members in nearly 100 countries.

Quiz

What is a dead zone?

a) a part of the ocean with so little oxygen that animals can't survive

b) a place where vampires and zombies hang out and party

c) a cemetery?

It's all connected

By now you've probably worked out that practically everything in this book is connected in some way. This means that one little thing you do can help Earth and its animals in lots of ways!

- If you cycle instead of drive, you help keep the air clean AND you reduce the greenhouse gases that are heating up the polar bears' Arctic homes.
- If you reuse your shopping bag, you save resources AND you keep plastic out of the environment where an animal might eat it.
- If you eat low on the food chain, you cut down on pollution AND you save water AND you discourage factory farming.

So remember, even a single action you take can have a big impact!

Get active

Congratulations! You're now a walking encyclopedia, full of knowledge about how to help the planet. You know how to eat and dress green. You know how to save energy, save water, and keep litter out of the environment. You know how to help animals, and how to make your school a more Earth-friendly place.

So what's left for an eco-genius like you to do? Take action! That includes reaching out to others to help make them as eco-aware as you are. If one person can do a lot, think of how much more a group can do!

Do you have a brilliant idea about how you and some friends can make your town greener? Is there one environmental issue that you're super-concerned about? Write a letter, raise some money, put up a website – there are zillions of ways you can help!

A park clean-up day is a fun way to help the planet and hang out with your friends.

96 Is there too much litter in a park or street near you? Get an adult's help, and organize a clean-up. Have a pizza party afterwards to celebrate.

97 When you visit a park or wildlife reserve, respect the plant life and animal life. Don't pick the plants, and don't do anything to annoy the animals. (You wouldn't want someone coming into your home and annoying you!)

98 Have a jumble sale or a cake sale to raise money for an environmental charity, such as Greenpeace or Rainforest Action Network.

99 Write a letter to the prime minister or your local member of parliament telling them how important it is that adults work to protect the environment. After all, kids can't do it all alone!

100 Write a play with your friends about a chosen environmental issue. Perform it for some younger kids.

Carwashing for friends and neighbours is a good way to raise money for an environmental charity. Just make sure you use a bucket instead of a hose to save water.

true story

Planet hero: Alec Loorz

When Alec Loorz was 12, he saw the movie *An Inconvenient Truth*, which describes the threat of climate change. Alec wanted to do something to help, so in 2007 he founded Kids vs Global Warming. The group educates other young people about climate change. Alec, who gives presentations to people of all ages, has won many awards for his work. He says,

"Lots of kids feel that they really can't make a difference. But I know that our voice matters more than anyone else's. We are the ones who will be most affected by what the world does or doesn't do NOW to change the way we use fossil fuels."

How to write a good letter

Want to make your voice heard? Writing a letter is a good way to start. You could send an email instead. But since writing an actual letter on paper takes more effort, letters tend to get more attention from decision-makers than emails.

Here are some letter-writing tips:

- Decide who should get your letter. If it's a local issue, you might want to write to a local councillor. If it's a national issue, you could write to your local member of parliament (MP).
- Put your own address and date at the top of the letter.
- Find out what address to send the letter to. You can do this online.
- Use the right greeting. "Dear MP" definitely won't work! Find out the person's name. Again, you can search online for this.
- In your letter, briefly say who you are and what you would like the person to do. Be polite!
- Check your spelling carefully, and make the letter as neat as you can. Write neatly, or type it on the computer and print it out.
- End with a polite closing, such as "Yours sincerely, (your name)" or "Yours truly, (your name)".
- Write out the envelope neatly, put on a postage stamp, and pop it in the letterbox!

101 Spread the word to, and set a good example for, younger children. It's hard to believe, but that little kid next door might be prime minister one day. Now that you're an expert on saving Earth, pass on some of your knowledge to younger kids. If you see them littering or wasting water, explain to them why they shouldn't. But be nice – no one likes getting lectured to or shouted at. If you have a younger brother or sister, perhaps they can help you do some of the things in this book. Our Earth needs all the help it can get!

"Nature is the original punk. Eco can be edgy, loud, fun, playful ... and hyper-cool. What's your punk?"

Linda Loudermilk, eco-fashion designer

Glossary

acid rain rain that has a higher than usual level of acid in it because of pollution

algae tiny plant-like organisms

carbon dioxide gas found in the air. Plants use it when making food and both plants and animals give it off when they breathe.

compost mixture of decomposing plants that can be used to enrich soil. Also, the act of making material into compost.

decompose break down or rot

deforestation cutting down trees

endangered species group of animals at risk of dying out

environment everything that surrounds a living thing

fertilizer substance that people use to help crops grow

fossil fuel material such as oil, coal, and natural gas that formed within Earth from plants and animals that lived millions of years ago

habitat place where an organism, such as an animal, lives

humus dark substance in soil that nourishes plants

insecticide substance used to kill insects

landfill disposal of waste by burying it

logging chopping down trees to be used as timber

non-renewable something, such as a natural resource, that cannot be replaced

nuclear power energy produced by splitting the atoms of certain materials

organic food grown without using artificial chemicals

overfishing taking too many fish from an area of the ocean

pesticide substance used to kill a pest

renewable something, such as a natural resource, that Earth cannot run out of

resource substance that is available for use

sustainable something, such as a natural resource, that Earth cannot run out of and that will not damage Earth

toxic poisonous

Find out more

Books

An Inconvenient Truth: The Planetary Emergency of Global Warming and What We Can Do About It, Al Gore (Bloomsbury Publishing, 2006)

Life Skills: Get Green!, Anne Marie Todd (Heinemann Library, 2009)

The Hot Topic: How to Tackle Global Warming and Still Keep the Lights On, David King and Gabrielle Walker (Bloomsbury Publishing, 2009)

The Little Book of Living Green, Mark Hegarty (Nightingale Press, 2007)

Why Science Matters: Predicting the Effects of Climate Change, John Townsend (Heinemann Library, 2009)

You Can Save The Planet, Rich Hough (A & C Black, 2007)

Websites

www.greenpeace.org/international/campaigns/oceans
This section of the Greenpeace website gives you information about by-catch, pollution, and over-fishing in the world's oceans.

www.worldwildlife.org
The website of the World Wildlife Fund has lots of information about how climate change is affecting animals and their habitats, as well as ways for you to get involved in campaigns.

www.gardenorganic.org.uk/schools_organic_network
Find out how to get your school involved in organic gardening.

www.ecofriendlykids.co.uk/EnergyRecyclingQuiz.html
Take the quiz on this website to test what you know about saving energy and recycling.

veggiekids.org.uk
Find some great advice about being a vegetarian on this website.

www.rootsandshoots.org

Visit the Roots & Shoots website to find out more about how you can get involved to help people, animals, and the environment around the world.

www.ryanswell.ca

Find out more about Ryan Hreljac and how he came to set up Ryan's Well Foundation on this website. You'll also find suggestions about how you can get involved in the struggle to bring clean water to people all over the world.

www.greenbeltmovement.org

Learn more about Wangari Maathai and the Green Belt Movement on this website. You can also pledge to plant a tree as part of the Billion Tree Campaign.

kids-vs-global-warming.com

Read about why Alec Loorz set up the Kids vs Global Warming website, as well as about the environmental projects his organization is taking part in.

Topics to research

- When you next pop into the supermarket, have a look around at the shelves. Which foods seem to have the most packaging? Which foods have the least? Can you think of ways in which people can reduce the number of packaged foods they buy?

- Many people drive cars rather than cycling, walking, or taking public transport. What are some reasons for this? Can you think of ways that cycling and taking public transport can be made easier, safer, and more fun?

- Choose an endangered animal species and learn more about it. Why is the species endangered? Are humans partly or wholly responsible? What steps can people take to help the species recover?

Index